God's Glory Poured Into My Story

Barbara J. Martin

Copyright © 2025 by Barbara J. Martin

All rights reserved. No part of this publication may be reproduced, distributed or transmitted in any form or by any means, including photocopying, recording, or other electronic or mechanical methods, without the prior written permission of the publisher, except in the case of brief quotations embodied in critical reviews and certain other noncommercial uses permitted by copyright law. For mission requests, write to the publisher, addressed " Attention: Permissions Coordinator," at the address below.

Barbara J. Martin/Rejoice Essential Publishing
PO BOX 512
Effingham, SC 29541
www.republishing.org

Unless otherwise indicated, scripture is taken from the King James Version.

God's Glory Poured into My Story/Barbara J. Martin

ISBN-13: 9798348599652

Dedication

I DEDICATE THIS BOOK TO everyone who has been reared by a grandparent, great-grandparent, or guardian other than their parents. To experience the love of a grandparent is an impressive experience.

Annie Mae Clark, my great-grandmother, your love was so amazing, and you were everything I needed as a child.

Ms. Alma J. Taylor, my birth mother, cared for my siblings (Cheryl Y. Shivers, Leonard McNair Jr., and Johnny F. Taylor) and I until she couldn't anymore due to sickness. Thank You for loving us enough and placing us in the care of our loving great-grandmother.

Dedication

Lillie Mae McCary, my great aunt, encouraged me by telling me to, "Fight on and be all that God would have me to be."

I dedicate this book to every person who has prayed, spoken strength into my life and inspired me to "Write."

I also dedicate this book to my entire family and Dwaine Moorman who was inspired by God to be a blessing for the vineyard of **KIDS KINGDOM LLC.**

I also dedicate this book to the memories of the late Emery Freeman and Lady Ruth Freeman who continues to be a vital part of my life. They are pioneers for the Gospel being shared across racial lines with love, whether in nursing homes, churches, or communities.

TABLE OF CONTENTS

ACKNOWLEDGEMENT..v
CHAPTER ONE: Vision of the Lord............1
CHAPTER TWO: It Is So..............................5
CHAPTER THREE: My Beginnings...............11
CHAPTER FOUR: Life Happens..................19
CHAPTER FIVE: God's Plans.....................22
CHAPTER SIX: Sunny Days.....................27
CHAPTER SEVEN: Leap of Faith..................31
ABOUT THE AUTHOR...38

Acknowledgement

Thank you, Holy Spirit, for imparting in me to author this book and now it has come to full fruition.

To Pastor Vernon Lloyd, an accomplished author, thank You for imparting into me to write my story.

God's Glory Poured into My Story

CHAPTER ONE

Vision Of The Lord

"*WRITE THE VISION, AND make it plain upon tables, that he may run that readeth it. For the vision is yet for an appointed time, but at the end it shall speak, and not lie: though it tarry, wait for it: because it will surely come, it will not tarry.*" — *(Habakkuk 2: 2-3)*

Have you ever been escorted to a center table in an elegant, breath-taking restaurant, then seated as all eyes take a glimpse at you? You have captured everyone's attention, and the surroundings are an awe-inspiring scene to behold. The table is set with the finest China, striking gold silverware, napkin folded, and a beautiful

God's Glory Poured into My Story

China cup turned upside down. I exhale in wonderment because everything is so exquisite.

In 2011, I had an open vision of the Lord, and it was as spectacular, and I recall it like yesterday. It was like an ordinary day, only to become a supernatural experience I'll never forget. I start every morning in prayer with God and on this day, I noted it to be a bit chilly. So, I decided to make a pot of coffee. Sitting at the table, I began to pour myself a cup of hot coffee. I then saw a cup tilted downward, smoke coming from it pouring onto the pages of a book. Holy Spirit spoke to me and said, "This is God's Glory pouring into the pages of the book you are to write. "Write Your Story!"

I continued to see this cup and the smoke. The cup felt fragile to the touch. It reminded me of expensive, fine porcelain and I felt as if my whole being began to sing, shout, and say aloud, "Hallelujah!" I saw God's glory as magnificent, weighty, priceless, and so genuine. Seeing His glory being poured out of that crystal cup with this amazing smoke and filling the atmosphere, my pores, veins, lungs, and all of me had me at a loss for words, and I shouted with a loud voice, Hallelujah!

Then, in 2024, thirteen years later, I brought my amazing story into fruition. God's vision is the metaphor and title for my book, *"God's Glory Poured into My Story."* As steam beams out of the cup, I saw the words, God's Glory, in a beautiful shade of red reminding me of the blood shed by our Savior on Calvary over two thousand years ago. The word "Poured" is gray colored like smoke filling the pages of my book, turning upward as though heaven was filling this book with words.

Then I saw the words, "Into My Story" in a deep purple, representing royalty through the eyes of God. Only God knows our real story and I believe that's why the page of the book is turned upward. The pouring of the smoke symbolizes God's presence and His hand in my life; the cup is me and how fragile we are and our need for Him, and the book is my life.

I'm reminded of the scripture, *Philippians 1:6, "Being confident of this very thing, that he*

God's Glory Poured into My Story

which begun a work in you will perform until the day of Jesus Christ." God was informing me that He was going to take me on a journey and will be with me throughout the entirety of the process. Despite what it may look like at times, the work in me will be finished. However, when the Holy Spirit reveals things to us, we must believe so we can receive and be absorbent like a sponge and soak it all in. Now, I'm ready to begin my story and I pray as you read this book that it will bring you joy, and peace, as your faith is renewed. *God's Glory Poured into My Story.*

CHAPTER TWO

It Is So

THIS THE THIRD TIME I am coming to you. In the mouth of two or three witnesses shall every word be established. — *(2 Corinthians 13:1 KJV)*

In 2011, little did I know that God had begun the process of my story. I was on a spiritual high because Sunday Morning service was fire and Apostle Kates' sermon was about faith in action, in reference to Joshua walking around the walls of Jericho. On the seventh time, the children of Israel shouted, and the walls collapsed. He then asked the congregation, "What do you want God to do for you?"

Later that evening, at home, I said within myself, "Lord, I would love to attend TD Jakes,

"*Woman Thou Art Loosed*" Conference in Texas." At 10 PM, my phone rang, which I found strange because of the lateness of the hour and I pondered, "Who is calling me?" I answered and it was a young lady who had just completed her internship at my facility, K.I.D.S. Kingdom LLC, as a teacher aide in early childhood education. She proceeded to tell me that every year since its inception she and her sister have attended the *"Woman Thou Art Loosed"* Conference together but won't be able to due to a death in the family. She said God told her to give her ticket to me.

I started shouting like Rhoda when she opened the door and saw Peter standing there (Acts 12). She got so excited because she saw the power of answered prayers. God had just supernaturally freed Peter from prison. God moved that quickly and the answer showed up at the door through a phone call. She told me I would be responsible for the airfare, travel, and hotel expenses. Can you believe it?

I was so flabbergasted. Look at God. I spoke it, and it manifested in a matter of hours. You can't tell me that prayer doesn't change things.

Job 22:28 says, "Thou shall also decree a thing, and it shall be established unto thee: and the light shall shine upon thy ways."

So after the phone call, I began to decree and declare, "Lord, you provided the seed, and you will provide the provision," and God did it. I called my friend Grace, who lived in Atlanta, to go with me, and she told me, "Barbara, it's for you to see God's glory." She agreed to pick me up and drive me to the airport. Once I arrived at the airport, I was immediately greeted by a male attendee who opened my car door, escorted me to the check-in line and stayed with me until I boarded the plane.

This experience was new to me and we now call it valet service. I was treated like royalty and had preferential treatment. I even asked him where his wife was because he treated me with so much class, as if he knew me. I flew Delta and on the plane, there was only one seat left and that was my ticket. I sat next to a doctor, and met a woman named Lois in a corresponding seat who was attending the conference as well.

God's Glory Poured into My Story

I arrived at Houston airport and proceeded to get a courtesy car to the hotel. Lois, the lady on the plane, came up to me and offered to give me a ride. I quickly prayed within myself, and God said it was safe to do so. This woman wasn't staying at the hotel and voluntarily picked me up and drove me back and forth from the hotel for the entire three days of the conference. We sat together during the conference.

Let me tell you how good my God is. When I tried to pay for my hotel with my check card that had money on it, it was denied so I had to use another card and there was no money in the account. The card was accepted, and I never got a bank letter for insufficient funds or a bank overdraft. All I can say is that God footed the bill.

When I arrived at the hotel to check in, there was only one room left, and it was at a priority level. The bellhop took my bags, and I rode the elevator to the eighth floor, and the doors opened to these large, beautiful glass doors. It was a floor by itself, a suite bigger than an apartment with full room service. I have never experienced anything like that in my entire life. I slept like a princess, and I was treated like one as well.

Friday night, Paula White was the speaker and while speaking, she stopped mid-sentence and said, "I don't know who this is for; someone here in this conference has a book inside of them, God's Glory poured into their story," and I screamed loudly, "That's for me," and this was the second confirmation. The next day after the conference concluded, Lois agreed to take me to the airport and before boarding the plane, I stopped at the gift shop and bought her a card and added cash inside, as an appreciation for her kindness towards me.

Lois sowed a book into me that her pastor wrote, and she told me, "One day you're going to write a book because you have your own story to write." In 2019, we had a guest speaker at my church and the minister told me, "There's a book inside of you and God is going to allow it to come to pass." God confirmed to me four times

God's Glory Poured into My Story

about this book and each time, I would be reassured. *God's Glory Poured into My Story.*

CHAPTER THREE

My Beginnings

RAIN UP A CHILD in the way he should go: and when he is old, he will not depart from it. —(Proverbs 22:6 KJV)

The definition of family may have several meanings, but one that I'm sure many will agree with and that is love. The collective love of family is so powerful and although we do not see and talk to each other, we know how to get together. Coming together is so uplifting and shows how God picks the family we're to be born in. He knows the family we need to become and fulfill what was ordained from the beginning of time. To God be the Glory!

God's Glory Poured into My Story

As I reminisce about my childhood, I realize there were some good and bad days. I was in an era of racial injustice called Jim Crow and people that looked like me often were sharecroppers or cotton pickers. We didn't possess much and anything we obtained came with much struggle. But love has a way of taking the sting, the pain.

I am the daughter of the late Alma J. Taylor of Eastman, Georgia, and she gave birth to four children. I am the second oldest and my siblings are Cheryl Y. Shivers, Leonard Mc Nair Jr., and Johnny F. Taylor. I was told as a child that my mother suffered from mental illness. The mental health system during this time was lacking and often, people were sent to a mental asylum.

My grandmother, Ms Ida Mae Blackshear, lived in Detroit, Michigan. She visited us on special days and would stay for a short period when we lived in Eastman, Georgia. She would bring each of us gifts and toys. These were gifts on our birthdays or at Christmas. When we moved to Dublin, Georgia, my memories of her are vague.

My Beginnings

My mother suffered with bouts of good days and bad days and when she had mental clarity, my siblings and 1 lived with her. She was very attentive and so loving. However, at other times, she wasn't functional and deemed incapable of caring for my siblings and I. So my great-grandmother, Annie Mae Clark, lived with us as my mother recuperated.

I ponder this scripture, *"God is a Father to the fatherless (Psalms 68:5 KJV)."* God proved His love for us repeatedly by providing a ram in the bush, which was my great-grandmother Annie, thus preventing my siblings and me from going into foster care. My great-grandmother was already up in age and sacrificed herself for us to ensure we had a safe place and be with family. It's through my great-grandmother that I saw unconditional love manifested in how she doted on us. She loved our wounds away with words of inspiration and affirming who I was in Christ and assisted us in welcoming our uniqueness and how to embrace it as strength.

We lived in a small town, and everybody knew each other's business. The children, adults, family, and strangers would talk about our mother in our presence. They called her crazy and we were labeled as Alma's kids in a condescending way. I cannot tell you how heart-wrenching it was to be treated that way. Not to mention how my great-grandmother was treated as well. Through it all, I can say my great-grandmother never lost her praise. People were swift to diagnose me as, "Oh, that's Alma's daughter," or "You're the daughter of crazy Alma." I was dismissed and often told I would never amount to anything.

As I got older, I could sympathize with Jesus when He was referred to, as the carpenter's son, and how he was not accepted in His own country (Matthew 13:55). The people could not get over the fact that he was from Nazareth, the ghetto and surely nothing good could come from such a place (John 1:46). Oh, but they were so wrong, Amen! Nazareth held a negative connotation then and when they referenced me as "Alma's daughter," word curses were spoken over me that I had to endure as a child and even into adulthood.

I suffered a lot of ugliness at the expense of people who should have known better, but my great-grandmother had a way of making me forget it all with a love that's indescribable: a grandmother's love. She did not have much, but what she had was Jesus, who was the greatest gift. Peter said, *"Silver and gold have I none but such as I have, I give thee Jesus (Acts 3:6)."*

My great-grandmother always had a smile on her face and a song in her heart. Every night, she would read her favorite chapter of the Bible to me, *Psalms 6*. Recently it was brought to my attention that she read to each of my siblings a different chapter also. She spoke many things into my life and there's one saying that I still hold onto today. Every night after reading me Psalms 6, she would tell me, "Barbara, you are a good child that will be misunderstood because people will not understand the genuine love you have for others. So, because of this, you will be used and hurt by some and misunderstood by others."

As an adult, I now comprehend what my great-grandmother meant. She never asked for much of my siblings and I, except that we love and treat people the way we wanted to be treated even when we were not treated right. These life lessons with her prepared me for life and I'm still gleaning from them today.

Lillie Mae McCary, my great aunt, my great grandmother's daughter, was once married but never had children. I became the child she never had and I was happy with that; one could never get enough love. Every summer I would be full of anticipation because I would spend the entire summer with her in Atlanta. I would ride the Greyhound bus, which was a big deal back then because, in my community, that was unheard of. Auntie had her own catering business and owned her home, which was out of the ordinary. I had my own room that was decorated so pretty and at home, no one had their own room. I was spoiled. Her dining room table was always displayed beautifully, and I couldn't take my eyes off it and she's who I got my ability to decorate.

In 1993, I called my auntie, who was now in her eighties, to tell her that I was coming to spend time with her for her birthday. Someone else answered the phone and informed me that they found her dead in the house. She was left to die. My auntie took care of her brother due to an illness until his death and for her die alone grieved me for a while. A family had befriended my auntie, and the daughter of the friend was a lawyer. She took my aunt's will and changed it. Instead of me getting everything, she got everything and because she was knowledgeable of the law, the will was legal and couldn't be challenged.

The bank allowed me to pay for her funeral expenses. I was permitted to take her bed, China cabinet and the dining table that I dearly loved in which I still possess today. Each time I look at it, I remember her and that can't be taken. Can you imagine never having children and working all your life to leave a loved one an inheritance in hopes of giving them a better life? You may ask, was I angry? Honestly, I was hurt. I cried, yelled. and at the same time, thanking God that my aunt didn't live to see the betrayal. The prayers of my great-grandmother and the word of God empowered me to let it go and let God have His way because vengeance is His and he

God's Glory Poured into My Story

will repay. So, I didn't become bitter but better. Praise God! *God Poured His Glory into My Story.*

CHAPTER FOUR

Life Happens

AND LO I AM with you always, even unto the end of the world. — (Matthew 28:20 KJV)

In January 1977, I was twenty-five years old and I met and married a handsome man named Gregory Martin, who was attending Tuskegee College with a major in engineering. He was a gentle, loving, and attentive husband and loving him was so easy. Greg left school after the death of his two brothers to be a support to his mother. He got a job at a local night club on the night shift. I lost two sons born prematurely before finally giving birth to a bundle of joy in 1980, my daughter Crystal. We were both proud parents and our smiles gleamed from ear to ear. God smiled on us with answered prayers and every time I held her in my arms and heard her little cry, God soothed me with the joy of motherhood. Her birth didn't replace my sons, but it comforted me and my husband.

In 1982, I received devastating and life altering news. My husband was shot and later died at the hospital. I was a newlywed and a young mother of a two year old. It was hard and I had no closure. I knew I couldn't quit or give up. I had no option because I had a daughter to raise with little to no support. I was able to wing it with prayers and the word of God.

Matthew 5:4 says, *"Blessed are they that mourn, for they shall be comforted."* I drew closer to God, and He drew closer to me. I know that it was God's grace that brought me through that difficult season of my life. I grieved in my own way. I became like Anna the Prophetess, who was a widow. She stayed at the temple offering up prayers and praise to God (Luke 2:36-40). In His presence, I gave Him all my pain and tears and was consoled. Just like my great-grandmother Annie, who never lost her praise, and I received the fullness of joy, and that joy gave me the strength to face every day.

In my pursuit of God's presence, I became a born again Christian and in 2012, I was called into the ministry as an Ambassador for Christ. In 2016, I was ordained an Evangelist under the leadership of Apostle Kenneth Kates and Elect Lady Ira Kates of *Christ Deliverance Temple* in Dublin, Georgia, serving faithfully as a Sunday School teacher and an Intercessor. Prophetess Anna witnessing Jesus as a baby was the fruit of her pain and prayers. What should have been a barren season for me became fruitful because my grief became a harvest of plenty. Look How *God Poured His Glory in My Story.*

CHAPTER FIVE

God's Plans

For I know the thoughts I think toward you, saith the Lord, thoughts of peace, and not of evil, to give you an expected end. — (Jeremiah 29:11)

In 1988 I wanted to make some extra money for the Christmas season. I was hired at Walmart and was promoted to store team leader. Twelve years later, in 2000, I was called to the management's office for a meeting. I didn't have any fear or dread because I knew I had excellent work ethics. *"And whatsoever you do, do it as unto the Lord, and not unto man (Colossians 3:23)."* Yes, it was a job, but I knew it was more than that. It was ministry and I was intentional with my actions. I seized every opportunity for Christ. I greeted everyone with a big smile.

God's Plans

I made sure they felt welcome. I shared Christ and encouraged countless customers. I became a living epistle, read and seen by all men by being a poster sign for Jesus.

In the office, I was offered a seat and I sat down. Across from me was the entire managerial team. One by one, they began to give accolades for doing a superb job. They noted that my work performance and productivity were superior, which was the making for a great leader. They offered me the assistance store manager position with the possibility of becoming a store manager. I was also informed that with this promotion, I would have to train at different Walmart locations throughout Georgia. I thanked God for the elevation, and I was humbled to be found worthy.

There's a cliché that say, "Favor ain't Fair." I would have to disagree because favor is fair because God is a just God. *"For promotion cometh neither from the east, nor from the west, nor from the south. But God is the judge he putteth down one, and setteth up another (Psalms 75:6-7)."* The promotion came with an exceptional packet and considerably above average salary back then. I told them I would get back to them because I had a lot to think about. I was a single mother with a preteen daughter and a limited support system. I didn't want to travel all over the state to train.

I prayed about it, and I sought the counsel of my friend, Mary. I told her that I wanted to own my own business, and that I wanted to be there for my daughter. I told her I think my answer is no. God reminded me of when I was a little girl. I would play boss with my cousins. I would dress up, carry a purse with my head lifted, and give them orders. I also recalled that Walmart was having staffing problems due to babysitting issues because many of the women were single moms.

God gave me a God-idea. I typed it up and it was sent to headquarters. I propose that a daycare be built in Walmart for their employees as a solution to alleviate staffing issues. The CEO, Sam Walton, looked at my proposal and he personally sent me a letter. He told me that he had contacted his legal team and concluded that it was a liability issue and that the risk was too great to take on this type of business investment. So, he unfortunately had to decline but congratulated me on suggesting a great idea and it was then that my passion for children was reignited. This inspired me to start a childcare business to meet the needs of the community.

So, after a few days, I informed management that I wasn't going to take the position because I wanted to start my own business in childcare. They were flabbergasted because they couldn't comprehend that I was turning down a definite source of income for a dream. They offered to give me more time, but I stood firm in my decision, and I knew it was the right thing to do. I had perfect peace and there was no fear in me. I was walking in blind faith and trusting in God. God told Abram to leave his family, the place of familiarity and to a place that had not yet been revealed to him (Genesis 12:1-3). God provided and fulfilled His promises, and Abram's identity changed to Abraham, a patriarch of faith and the Father Of Many Nations. Obedience and faith always bring increase and favor.

God's Glory Poured into My Story

In 2000, I registered at Oconee Fall Line College and it was all faith and much prayer. I was given financial aid and Pell grants. There were times when someone paid my tuition and people would give me checks. I didn't tell anyone about the financial strain I was encountering, but God knew. *"My God shall supply all your need according to His riches in glory in Christ Jesus (Philippians 4:19)."* I graduated with an Associate Degree in Early Childcare and Education. *God Poured His Glory into My Story.*

CHAPTER SIX

Sunny Days

"*THOU HAS TURNED MY mourning into dancing: thou has put off my sackcloth and girded me with gladness.*" — *(Psalms 30:11 KJV)*

My mother was placed in a twenty-four-hour care facility at Southland Rehabilitation Center in Dublin, Georgia, in 2005 until her passing in 2013. It's a paradox. After she became ill, we began to have interesting and heart-felt conversations. From her hospital bed, she imparted wisdom and counsel into me. The little girl in me needed her, and from her bed, she was rearing me. I really enjoyed our one-on-one time together, and years later, I realized that God was redeeming the time for us both.

The little girl Barbara, now an adult, needed the love of her mother, and my mom needed the love of her daughter. She told me that she could discern the sound of my footsteps. Isn't that beautiful? God has a wondrous way of making things beautiful in His time. She would often say how proud she was of me being a successful business owner with two childcare locations. I learned valuable lessons from her during those visits, and that is how to endure in your hour of crushing. There were occasions when I could discern that her body was riddled with pain with her facial expressions, but my mother never complained. She continued to smile and welcome our times together.

God said, *"And I will restore to you the years that the locust hath eaten, the cankerworm, and the caterpillar, and the palmerworm, my great army which I sent among you (Joel 2:25 KJV)."*

We have a God that, in all His infinite wisdom, God our Father, knew I needed all those years I lost as a child with my mother due to her mental illness. I was able to get an overload of my mother's love which I hold dearly and will never forget. After the passing of my mother in 2013, I was left with a great void in my life because I deeply missed talking to her and those visits made my day. My business was at an all-time low due to the economy and the transition in staffing that continued for weeks. I was so dry; I had nothing to give, and I had no inclination in what to do. I was in a valley of dry bones and I began to cry to God. I asked the Holy Spirit to give me a reason to continue and to restore unto me the joy of my salvation, and my passion to live. For my days had become so cloudy and my faith was like gas fumes, non-existent. I couldn't hear the voice of God no matter how much I sought him like Elijah, who suddenly heard the still small voice of God (1 Kings 19:11-13).

In 2014, I experienced a suddenly. My life was never the same but better and blessed. I was given a new reason to live and to share my love with someone who needed it. Love has no boundaries, and she is my adorable granddaughter, Sunjai Simmons, a beautiful talented, intelligent, and tech savvy girl. She excels academically and is an honor student at Irish Gifted Academy. She is loved by everyone and has a loving spirit.

God's Glory Poured into My Story

She's quick to let everyone know that she's the assistant CEO of K.I.D.S. Kingdom LLC and is a great support to me. Oh, what an amazing God!

Psalms 91:1-2 says, *"He that dwelleth in the secret place of the Most High shall abide under the shadow of the Almighty. Oh, he will cover us with his feathers and under his wings do I trust."*

God Poured His Glory into My Story.

CHAPTER SEVEN

Leap of Faith

AITH IS THE SUBSTANCE of things hoped for, and the evidence of things not seen. — (Hebrews 11:1 KJV)

After graduating from college in 2003, I started Bows and Bowties, a childcare business in my home with six children. Oconee College, the college I attended, gave me a business grant and donated all the equipment I needed to start my business. After three years, with my business flourishing, I was led by God to look for a commercial building. He was telling me that the vision was bigger and needed more room to do it. I looked at a building and as I was walking through it and I saw the layout was formerly a cellphone business. I had to transform it into a childcare facility.

So, in 2006, K.I.D.S. Kingdom LLC, a childcare service on 517 Telfair Street in Dublin, Georgia, was established. We provide services for babies from six weeks to twelve years of age. God told me that it would be a beacon of light to the community. "You will educate the children, and the children will elevate" according to *Isaiah 54:13*. The children, after leaving our center, will then go to Pre-K and sometimes some go straight to kindergarten. Also, we provided an after-school program, where children can come and do their homework.

In 2012, I opened a second location, K.I.D.S. Kingdom Academy, on 1000 Telfair Street, by leasing a building that was used for children with behaviors. The layout was perfect for the vision and it's as if it was done specifically for me. God is so good because it was a turnkey blessing and God told me I would have two locations. A childcare center accepting babies at six weeks to school age, providing childcare, and school in a caring, safe, and engaging environment where they can grow and flourish under the supervision of nurturing care of highly skilled teachers.

All the teachers and teacher assistants are educated in Early Childhood education and my business is an accredited entity. Our curriculum meets the individual requirements of young learners, offering children a variety of activities that are fun, and thought-provoking learning. Yearly, the school superintendent continues to recognize my business as top tier in advanced learning because the children know their colors, shapes, numbers, and alphabets and some were able to print their names. All this is achieved before entering pre-school and some have been able to go straight to kindergarten.

In 2023, K.I.D.S. Kingdom LLC was asked to say the Pledge Of Allegiance on National Prayer Day at the Farmer's market in Dublin. The kids were so proud. They articulated every word loud and clear in a spirit of excellence. When you are obedient to what God has ordained, He'll shine His glory upon it. Those kids were like a lighthouse beaming bright that unbeknownst to me, they touched the heart of a philanthropist in the audience.

One day after opening the center for the day, an unknown man visited the center and he said he saw kids' performance at the market and was so impressed and wanted to sow into the vision of K.I.D.S. Kingdom LLC. He then presented me with a check in a substantial amount. When you hear that we entertain angels unaware, believe it! God knew this blessing was so needed and right on time. An eighteen-wheeler truck hit and ran into the building sign and the city wasn't responsible for the repairs and through insurance, I still had to pay a large amount out of pocket. This was also during the holidays and funding for Covid ended and I wanted to pay my staff before the holidays and not afterwards.

However, I'm thankful that it happened during closure hours and didn't hit the building itself. Every day since I have been given Psalms 91, I walk around the center declaring it and I believe because of this, the truck hit only the sign and missed the building. Hallelujah!

According to *Isaiah 43:15-16*, *"I am the Lord, your Holy One, the creator of Israel, your King; Thus saith the Lord, which maketh a way in the sea, and a path in the mighty waters."* God is a Way Maker. When it's His vision, He will provide the provision. Through countless testimonies I can tell of how people volunteered to cut the grass, donations, etc. When I think of the goodness of Jesus, my soul cries out, "Hallelujah!" All it took was a little faith like the grain of a mustard seed and a yes in my heart. God took that and multiplied it. My yes broke word curses spoken over me such as, "I'll never amount to anything, I'm just like Alma or Oh, that's Alma's daughter or That's crazy Alma's daughter." It also continues to break barriers as a Black woman. To God be the glory, everything does have a way of working out for our good and what the enemy thought would kill, delay, and deny me.

Obedience also brings favor and in 2023, I was recognized and awarded a Community and Leadership Award for Dublin and in 2024, an Alumni for Oconee Falls Line College, from which students do their internship at Kingdom K.I.D.S. LLC. Today I have been blessed to be an entrepreneur and owner of a thriving business in childcare for twenty-two years and counting. I have broken many barriers as a successful Black woman. I am a sought-out speaker sharing the message of faith through my testimony that encourages the saints of God to take a leap of faith and start those kingdom businesses. The future of Kingdom K.I.D.S. LLC is bright and will continue to meet the needs of the children and provide a source of income for the community.

In the future, we will expand the building with additional spaces and add a small building where I can teach the word of God to women. I will continue to evangelize the word of God over the airways through my radio ministry titled, Secret Place" teaching Psalms 91, which was started in 2017. God told me to go to the radio station WMLT and an empty slot had just become available, and the next Sunday, I was on the air from 7:45 am to 8 am. In 2021, my time increased to 7 am to 7:30 am every Sunday. If I were to sum up my life, my anthem would be the song, "I Come This Far by Faith Leaning on the Lord's Side." God did this for me! I will forever be at His feet! God's Glory Poured into My Yes,

today. I am proud to be called Alma's daughter.
He has Poured His Glory Into My Story.

About The Author

Barbara J. Martin, the daughter of the late Ms. Alma J. Taylor, was born in Eastman, Dodge County, Georgia. She has three siblings: Cheryl Y. Shivers, Leonard McNair Jr., and Johnny F. Taylor. She is a delighted parent to one daughter, Mrs. Crystal Martin Jackson and a beautiful granddaughter, Miss Sunjai Simmons. She is a graduate of Oconee Fall Line College with an associate in early Childcare and Education. She is a born-again Christian and member of the Christ Deliverance Temple Church, under the leadership of Apostle Kenneth Kates and Elect Lady Ira Kates.

About The Author

In 2012, she was called into the ministry as an Ambassador of Christ. In 2016, she was ordained as an Evangelist by Apostle Kenneth Kates. She's a Sunday School teacher and has a radio ministry called "Secret Place," which airs every Sunday at 7 AM. She is the CEO of K.I.D.S Kingdom LLC and K.I.D.S Kingdom Academy.

Index

A

Abraham, 25
adulthood, 14
airfare, 6
airport, 7, 8, 9
Alma J. Taylor, 12, 38
Ambassador, 21, 39
angels, 34
Anna the Prophetess, 20
Annie Mae Clark, 13
Apostle Kenneth Kates, 21, 38, 39
Atlanta, 7, 16
atmosphere, 2
aunt, 16, 17

B

babies, 32
bank, 8, 17

Index

bank overdraft, 8
Barbara, 7, 15, 28
bellhop, 8
betrayal, 17
Bible, 15
birthdays, 12
bitter, 18
Black woman, 35, 36
blood, 3
book, 2, 3, 4, 9, 10
boss, 24
brother, 17
business, 13, 16, 24, 25, 28, 29, 31, 32, 33, 36

C

Calvary, 3
car, 7, 8
check card, 8
Cheryl Y. Shivers, 12, 38
child, 11, 12, 14, 15, 16, 28
childhood, 6, 12
children, 5, 12, 13, 16, 17, 25, 31, 32, 33, 36
China, 1, 2, 17
Christ Deliverance Temple Church, 38
Christian, 21, 38

Christmas, 12, 22
church, 9
coffee, 2
community, 16, 25, 32, 36
Community and Leadership Award, 35
Conference, 6
congregation, 5
cotton pickers, 12
cousins, 24
Covid, 34
cup, 2, 3
customers, 23

D

daughter, 12, 14, 16, 17, 19, 20, 24, 28, 35, 37, 38
daycare, 24
death, 6, 17, 19
Delta, 7
Detroit, Michigan, 12
doctor, 7
Dublin, Georgia, 12, 21, 27, 32

E

early childhood education, 6

Eastman, Georgia, 12
economy, 29
Elect Lady Ira Kates, 21, 38
elevator, 8
Elijah, 29
entrepreneur, 36
epistle, 23
Evangelist, 21, 39

F

facility, 6
faith, 4, 5, 25, 26, 29, 35, 36
family, 6, 11, 13, 17, 25
favor, 23, 25, 35
fear, 22, 25
foster care, 13
funeral expenses, 17

G

ghetto, 14
gifts, 12
girl, 24, 27, 28, 29
Glory, 2, 3, 4, 9, 10, 11, 18, 21, 26, 30, 36, 37

God, 2, 3, 4, 5, 6, 7, 8, 9, 10, 11, 13, 17, 18, 19, 20, 21, 22, 23, 24, 25, 26, 27, 28, 29, 30, 31, 32, 33, 34, 35, 36
Grace, 7
granddaughter, 29, 38
grandmother, 12, 13, 14, 15, 16
great leader, 23
great-grandmother, 13, 14, 15, 17, 20
Gregory Martin, 19
Greyhound bus, 16
grief, 21

H

headquarters, 24
heart, 14, 15, 27, 34, 35
holidays, 34
Holy Spirit, 2, 4, 29
hospital, 20, 27
hotel, 6, 8
husband, 19, 20

I

illness, 17
inspiration, 13

Index

insurance, 34
Intercessor, 21
internship, 6, 35
Irish Gifted Academy, 29
Israel, 5, 35

J

Jericho, 5
Jesus, 4, 14, 15, 21, 23, 26, 35
Jesus Christ, 4
Jim Crow, 12
job, 19, 22, 23
Johnny F. Taylor, 12, 38
Joshua, 5
journey, 4
joy, 4, 19, 20, 21, 29

K

K.I.D.S. Kingdom Academy, 32
K.I.D.S. Kingdom LLC, 6, 30, 32, 33, 34
kindergarten, 32, 33

L

lady, 6, 8
lawyer, 17
Leonard Mc Nair Jr, 12
life, 3, 9, 15, 16, 17, 20, 29, 36
lighthouse, 33
Lillie Mae McCary, 16
Lois, 7, 8, 9
Lord, 1, 2, 5, 7, 22, 35, 36
love, 5, 11, 12, 13, 15, 16, 28, 29
lungs, 2

M

Mary, 24
meeting, 22
memories, 12
mental asylum, 12
mental health system, 12
mental illness, 12, 28
minister, 9
ministry, 21, 22, 36, 39
money, 8, 22
mother, 12, 13, 14, 19, 20, 24, 27, 28, 29
motherhood, 20
Mrs. Crystal Martin Jackson, 38
Ms Ida Mae Blackshear, 12

Index

mustard seed, 35

N

napkin, 1
Nazareth, 14

O

Obedience, 25, 35
Oconee College, 31
Oconee Fall Line College, 26, 38

P

pain, 12, 20, 21, 28
parents, 19
pastor, 9
Paula White, 9
peace, 4, 22, 25
Pell grants, 26
people, 12, 14, 15, 16, 26, 35
Peter, 6, 15
phone, 6, 7, 16
phone call, 6, 7
plane, 7, 8, 9

Pledge Of Allegiance, 33
pores, 2
praise, 14, 20
prayer, 2, 6, 26
prayers, 6, 17, 19, 20, 21
princess, 9
prison, 6
promotion, 23
provision, 7, 35
purse, 24

R

radio station, 36
restaurant, 1
Rhoda, 6
royalty, 3, 7

S

Sam Walton, 24
Savior, 3
scripture, 3, 13
Secret Place, 36, 39
sermon, 5
sharecroppers, 12

Index

siblings, 12, 13, 15, 38
silverware, 1
sister, 6
smile, 15, 22, 28
smoke, 2, 3
Southland Rehabilitation Center, 27
store manager, 23
Story, 2, 3, 4, 10, 18, 21, 26, 30, 37
Sunjai Simmons, 29, 38
supernatural, 2

T

tables, 1
TD Jakes, 5
teacher, 6, 21, 33, 39
Texas, 6
ticket, 6, 7
time, 1, 5, 10, 11, 12, 16, 17, 20, 25, 27, 28, 29, 34, 36
toys, 12
travel, 6, 24
truck, 34
tuition, 26
Tuskegee College, 19

V

veins, 2
vision, 1, 2, 3, 31, 32, 34, 35
voice, 3, 29

W

Walmart, 22, 23, 24
Way Maker, 35
widow, 20
wife, 7
wisdom, 27, 28
WMLT, 36

www.ingramcontent.com/pod-product-compliance
Lightning Source LLC
LaVergne TN
LVHW020416070526
838199LV00054B/3628